DATE DUE

JAN 0 4 '05			

Exploring Space

By Gregory Vogt

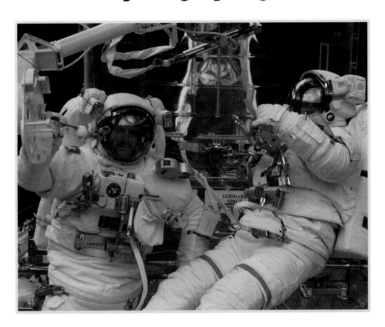

Steadwell Books

Raintree Steck-Vaughn Publishers

A Harcourt Company

Austin · New York

www.steck-vaughn.com

OUR UNIVERSE

Published by Raintree Steck-Vaughn Publishers, an imprint of Steck-Vaughn Company.

Library of Congress Cataloging-in-Publication Data
Vogt, Gregory.
    Exploring Space/by Gregory Vogt.
        p.cm. (Our universe)
    Includes index.
    ISBN 0-7398-3113-5
    1. Space exploration--Juvenile literature. [1. Space exploration.] I. Title.

Printed in the United States of America
10 9 8 7 6 5 4 3 2 1 LB 02 01 00

Produced by Compass Books

Photo Acknowledgments
All photographs courtesy of NASA.

Content Consultant
Dr. David Jewitt
Professor of Astronomy
University of Hawaii Institute for Astronomy

Contents

Diagram of a Space Shuttle

Flight Deck
—an area for the pilot and the space shuttle controls

Cargo Bay
—a place where objects the shuttle carries into space are kept

Spacelab
—a laboratory where astronauts do experiments

Main Engines
—machines that fire on liftoff to push the shuttle into space

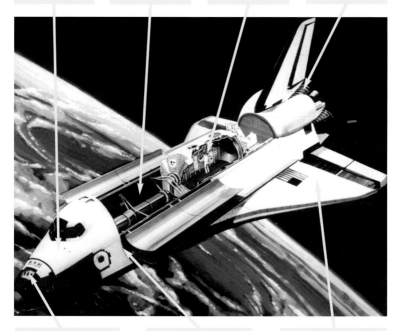

Small Rockets
—devices that help the shuttle move and change its path

Lower Deck
—an area where the astronauts live and work

Wings
—parts the shuttle uses to glide through Earth's atmosphere to its landing site

How do people travel into space?
People ride in spacecraft that are pushed into space by powerful rockets.

What kind of spacecraft do astronauts ride in?
Today, many astronauts travel into space in a space shuttle. This reuseable spacecraft looks like an airplane.

How do people survive in space?
Spacecraft supply astronauts with air, food, and other things necessary to survive.

How do astronauts survive outside of spacecraft?
Astronauts wear spacesuits when they leave their spacecraft. The spacesuit protects them from deadly energy waves in space. It also keeps them warm. Tanks on the back of the suit provide air for astronauts to breathe.

What other worlds have people visited?
People have landed on the Moon. But they have not yet visited any other planets.

These rockets are pushing a spacecraft into space.

Rocket Power

For thousands of years, people have wondered what other worlds in space are like. Some people in ancient times dreamed of exploring space. But they had no way of traveling there.

In about 1100 B.C., Chinese people invented the rocket. This tubelike device travels very fast. Early Chinese rockets were bamboo tubes. The front end of the tube was closed. The back end of the tube was open. People filled the open end of the tube with gunpowder. To fire the rocket, people lit the gunpowder. This caused a small explosion. The force of the explosion pushed the rocket forward.

Over the years, people have found many uses for rockets. Rockets carry fireworks into the air. During war, people use rockets to carry weapons. And powerful rockets can even push objects into space.

About Space Rockets

Today, there is only one way to travel into space. People must use rockets. The basic rocket for space travel is a long tube. The top end of the tube is usually pointed. The pointed design makes the rocket travel through the air easily.

Rocket engines are on the bottom end of the tube. Early rockets had one engine. Modern rockets have three or more engines.

Some rockets have stabilizers. Stabilizers are wings shaped like fins. They are on the bottom of the rocket. Stabilizers help balance the rocket.

Rockets carry things like satellites and space capsules into space. A satellite is a spacecraft that circles Earth. A space capsule is a small bell-shaped spacecraft. The things rockets carry are called payloads.

Inside the rocket tube is fuel. Rocket engines can run on several types of fuel. Early rockets used solid fuel, such as gunpowder. Modern rockets use liquid fuel, such as liquid oxygen and liquid hydrogen. Some rockets use more than one kind of fuel. Using a combination of different fuels gives the rocket more power.

During blastoff, the fuel is ignited, or set on fire, and the engines are powered. This causes flames and gas from the engines to rush out of nozzles, or tubes,

▲ **This is a photo of the space shuttle blasting off into space.**

at the bottom end of the rocket. The superheated gases speed out and push against the ground. This pushes the rocket upward.

Rockets are fired off from a launch pad. A launch pad is a safe area away from people and buildings. The noise from a rocket launch could damage people's hearing. Sometimes an accident or a faulty rocket might explode.

▲ **Rockets need a great deal of thrust to push spacecraft into space.**

Why Rockets Work

Rocket designs are based on the three laws of motion. English scientist Sir Isaac Newton first stated these laws in 1687.

The first law says that an object's motion remains constant, or the same. A moving object keeps moving until something stops it. Something that is sitting still stays still unless an outside force pushes it and puts it in motion. A rocket needs the force produced by its engines to lift it.

Another law says that every action has an equal and opposite reaction. For example, the burned fuel shoots downward out the bottom of the rocket. This action creates an opposite reaction. The fuel's downward force pushes the rocket upward.

The last law says that the greater the force, the more an object will move. It also explains that a heavier object needs greater force to move it. For example, if a person pushes an empty swing gently, the swing does not move much. But if the person pushes harder, the swing moves more. The person must push even harder if someone is sitting on the swing.

Rockets use fuel as their push. They burn a great deal of fuel very quickly. Gas and fire speed out of nozzles in the bottom of the rocket. This creates a lot of force called thrust. Thrust pushes rockets forward very quickly.

Rockets need greater thrust when they carry heavy payloads into space. The heavier the payload, the greater the thrust the payload needs to send it into space. Scientists may use large rockets or several rockets at one time to create more thrust.

 Scientists test rocket engines to make sure they work well.

Robert H. Goddard

American scientist Robert H. Goddard is nicknamed the "father of rocket technology." In the early 1900s, he made many changes and improvements to rocket designs. He wanted to create rockets that were powerful enough to carry astronauts to the Moon.

Goddard changed the type of fuel used in rockets. Early rockets all used solid fuel. But Goddard believed that liquid fuel could provide more power. He also believed liquid-fueled rockets could travel all the way to the Moon.

Goddard made a rocket with an upside-down design. The engine was at the top and pointed downward. He made a fuel tank to hold liquid fuel and attached it to the bottom of the engine. Based on Newton's second law of motion, the force flowing out of the bottom of the engine would push the rocket up.

In 1926, Goddard fired the rocket. It climbed to 60 feet (18 m). Goddard improved his rocket design. Some of his rockets climbed thousands of feet. Today, liquid fuel is used in most rockets that reach space.

Stages

Scientists build modern rockets in parts called stages. Each stage falls away when it is no longer needed. This makes the rocket lighter, so the engines in the remaining stages can make it go even faster.

Most rockets have a three-stage design. The first stage lifts the rocket from the ground. It falls off when it runs out of fuel. The second stage carries the rocket higher into the atmosphere. The atmosphere is a layer of gas surrounding an object in space. The second stage also falls off when it is out of fuel. Then the third stage takes the rocket where it is going.

This picture was taken from the inside of the space shuttle while it was in space. It shows the cargo bay where the payload is kept.

Missiles and Spacecraft

Missiles were the first rockets used for space travel. A missile is a long rocket that carries a weapon on its upper end. Scientists design missiles to be aimed at enemy targets. To reach its target, the missile travels very high above Earth in a curved path. At the top of the curve, the missile begins to travel down toward its target.

Scientists realized that missiles were just right for traveling through space. During its early space

Astronauts on Board

The first capsule used for sending astronauts into space was the *Mercury* capsule. It could hold only one astronaut. The *Gemini* capsule came next. It held two astronauts. The *Apollo* capsule (above) held three astronauts. The *Space Shuttle Orbiter* can hold up to eight astronauts. The *Orbiter* is like an airplane. Two rockets sit on both sides of the *Orbiter*. The rockets push the *Orbiter* into space. The *Space Shuttle Orbiter* is the first reusable spacecraft.

program, the United States used missiles to carry payloads into space.

Missiles carried the first satellites into orbit around Earth. Satellites have many uses. They gather information, send information, and take pictures.

Missiles also launched the first astronauts into space. Astronauts sat inside a capsule. Up to three astronauts could fit inside a space capsule. The rocket pushed the capsule into space. When it returned to Earth, the capsule splashed down into the ocean. A ship was sent to pick up the astronauts.

Scientists still use missiles to send spacecraft into space. But U.S. astronauts ride the space shuttle now instead of capsules. The space shuttle is a reusable airplanelike spacecraft designed for astronauts.

This is an artist's drawing of *Mariner 2*. It
was the first spacecraft to fly by a planet.

Early Space Missions

In 1962, scientists launched a missile with an important payload. The payload was a space probe called *Mariner 2*. A space probe is a spacecraft built to explore and gather information about space. *Mariner 2*'s mission was to travel to Venus to study the planet. At the time, no space probe had visited Venus.

Mariner 2 traveled above Earth and then headed out into space. The space probe traveled 48,000 miles (77,249 km) and passed 22,000 miles (35,406 km) away from Venus.

Mariner 2 was the first spacecraft to successfully reach another planet. It measured Venus's temperature. It also studied Venus's clouds and measured other things about the planet. *Mariner 2* proved that machines could be space explorers.

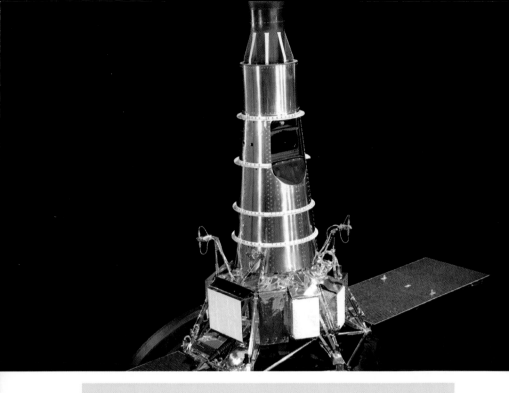

▲ This is an artist's drawing of a *Ranger*. Before it crashed, it took pictures of the Moon.

Going to the Moon

One of the early goals of the U.S. space program was to send humans to the Moon. The Moon is a rocky ball that is 2,159 miles (3,475 km) in diameter. Diameter is the distance through the center of a circle. The Moon is an average of 238,600 miles (384,400 km) from Earth.

Planning the Moon mission was difficult. Scientists knew the journey to the Moon would be long and dangerous. Astronauts would travel many thousands of miles to get there. They would be in space for a week or more. Then they would need a way to land on the Moon.

Astronauts would also need spacesuits to protect themselves on the Moon's surface. Spacesuits keep astronauts' bodies at the right temperatures. The suit's fabric protects the body from harmful sun rays. Tanks on the back of the suits provide oxygen for the astronauts to breathe.

Scientists did not know if conditions on the Moon were dangerous. Some people thought there might be huge pools of dust like quicksand. So scientists sent spacecraft to the Moon before the astronauts went.

Beginning in the late 1950s, three different kinds of spacecraft went to the Moon. *Ranger* spacecraft carried television cameras. The cameras took close-up pictures of the Moon's surface and sent them back to Earth. The pictures showed no liquid water on the Moon. Instead, dustlike soil and light gray and black rocks covered the ground.

Surveyor spacecraft had rocket engines and legs. They landed on the Moon and did not find any dust pools.

Lunar Orbiters circled the Moon. They took pictures of possible landing sites for the astronauts.

▲ **Apollo astronauts put a U.S. flag on the Moon when they landed.**

Apollo Missions

Apollo was the name of the space program in charge of sending astronauts to the Moon. Scientists designed special spacecraft for these missions. Each *Apollo* spacecraft had two parts.

The first part was a command module. A module is a conelike capsule. The astronauts lived in the command module during the mission. It was built to stay in orbit around the Moon and then return to Earth.

The lunar module was the second part of the *Apollo* spacecraft. Scientists designed it to land on the Moon. It had four legs and a large engine for landing. The lander was attached to the command module. It separated from the module to land on the Moon.

There were nine human missions to the Moon during the Apollo program. Each mission had a different job to do. *Apollo 8* was the first Apollo mission with people aboard to orbit the Moon. The astronauts in *Apollo 10* practiced using the lander. An astronaut took the lander to 10 miles (16 km) above the Moon, and then returned to the command module.

People first landed on the Moon during the *Apollo 11* mission. To do this, scientists built the largest rocket in the world. The *Saturn V* rocket was about 363 feet (111 m) tall. Three astronauts rode in a capsule at the top of the rocket. These astronauts were Neil Armstrong, Michael Collins, and Edwin Aldrin, Jr.

On July 16, 1969, *Apollo 11* launched from the Kennedy Space Center in Florida. *Apollo 11* traveled for three days before it entered the Moon's orbit. Then Armstrong and Aldrin climbed into the lander. Collins stayed in the command module above the Moon. On July 20, 1969, Armstrong and Aldrin landed on the Moon. They put on spacesuits and walked outside. They collected rocks to bring home.

This is an artist's drawing of *Mariner 10* in space. It took many pictures of Mercury.

Mariner 10 to Venus and Mercury

One of the great explorer space probes was *Mariner 10*. It was launched in 1973. A few months later, it passed by Venus. It flew 3,600 miles (5,794 km) above Venus's cloud tops. While there, it measured wind speeds and temperature. It found that high clouds on Venus looked like clouds on Earth.

Until *Mariner 10*, no other space probe had ever been to Mercury. *Mariner 10* flew by Mercury three times before it ran out of fuel. Cameras on *Mariner 10* took pictures and used computers to send them back to Earth.

The pictures showed that Mercury looks like Earth's Moon. It has many craters, or bowl-shaped holes. Meteorites crashed into Mercury and blasted the craters. Meteorites are pieces of space rock and metal that crash into objects in space.

Magellan

Even after *Mariner 10*, scientists still knew little about Venus. Venus's clouds surrounded the planet and blocked the view of its surface. Scientists needed a special kind of space probe to see the whole surface.

In 1989, the United States sent the *Magellan* space probe to Venus. *Magellan* carried a radar machine. Radar bounces radio waves off a surface. Radio waves are a form of energy that can travel through clouds.

Magellan used radar to map 98% of the surface of Venus. It sent radio waves downward and then caught them when they bounced back. The waves told scientists how far down the surface was and how the land was shaped. Scientists found thousands of volcanoes on Venus. *Magellan* orbited Venus until it stopped working in 1994.

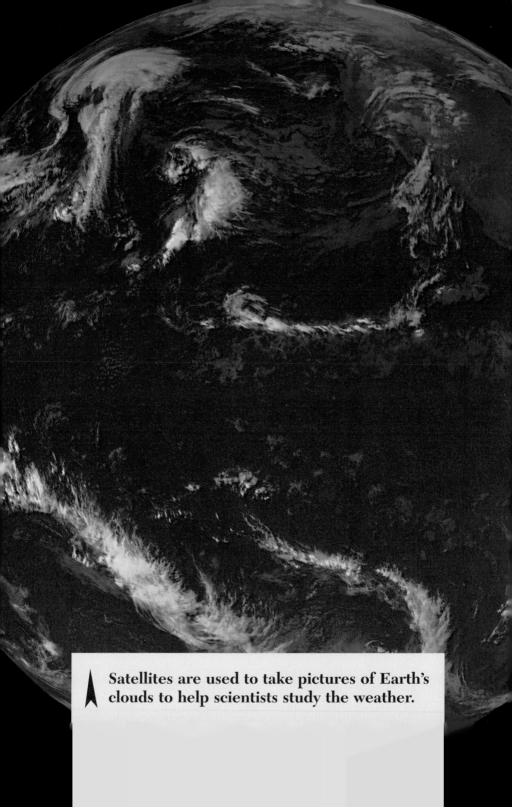

Satellites are used to take pictures of Earth's clouds to help scientists study the weather.

Artificial Earth Satellites

People cannot see much of Earth at one time because they live on its surface. Many artificial satellites have been sent above Earth to give people a view they cannot see from the ground. Artificial means made by humans. Each satellite has its own job. Some satellites take pictures or record information about Earth. Other satellites send TV or radio signals around the planet.

Weather satellites take pictures of Earth's clouds. Meteorologists look at these pictures. Meteorologists are scientists who study the weather. The pictures help them predict the weather. For example, swirling clouds over the Atlantic Ocean warn of a hurricane. Wide, dark clouds mean rain is coming. Weather satellites are also used to measure rainfall and wind speeds.

The *Landsat* satellites take pictures of Earth's land. Scientists look at the pictures to learn about how land is used. They learn about pollution, crops, and where to look for minerals. They also make maps based on the pictures.

Ocean satellites help scientists observe currents, or how water flows. Studying currents, such as El Niño, helps scientists predict changes in Earth's climate.

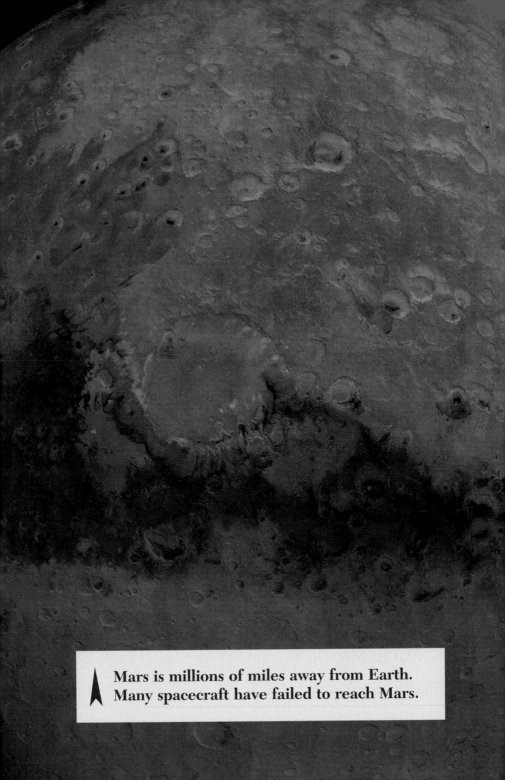

Mars is millions of miles away from Earth. Many spacecraft have failed to reach Mars.

Flights to Mars

Mars is about 35 million miles (56 million km) away from Earth at the closest point in its orbit. The surface of Mars looks fuzzy even through very powerful telescopes. Scientists must send space probes to Mars to see what the planet really looks like. The space probes send pictures of Mars back to scientists on Earth.

More than 30 spacecraft have been sent to Mars. Only about half of those survived the trip there.

Mars 1 was the first space probe scientists tried to send to Mars. On November 1, 1962, *Mars 1* took off from the Soviet Union. Scientists lost radio contact with the spacecraft. The mission failed.

In 1964, scientists in the United States tried to send a space probe to Mars. *Mariner 3* had problems, too. It also failed to reach Mars.

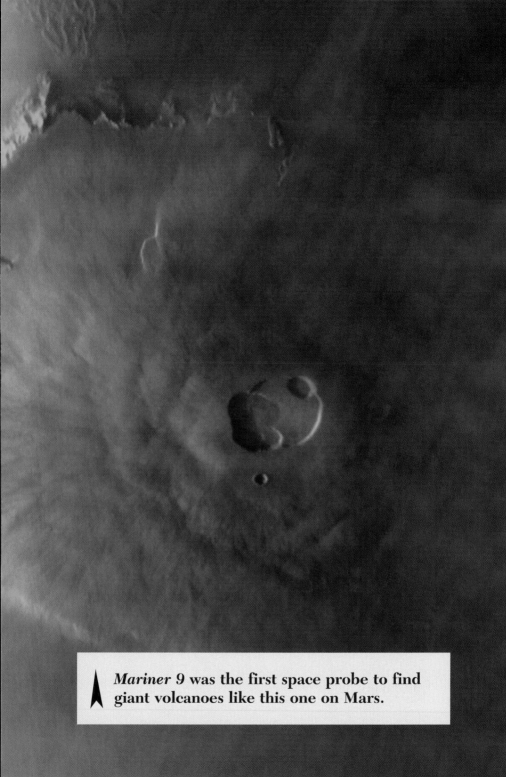

Mariner 9 was the first space probe to find giant volcanoes like this one on Mars.

Successful *Mariner* Missions

On November 28, 1964, U.S. scientists launched the *Mariner 4* spacecraft. Its mission was a success. It flew past Mars on July 15, 1965. As it flew by Mars, it snapped many close-up pictures of the planet's surface.

Two more U.S spacecraft made the trip to Mars in 1969. *Mariner 6* took 75 pictures of Mars. *Mariner 7* took 126 pictures.

The United States sent *Mariner 9* to orbit Mars in 1971. When it began orbiting, a big dust storm covered the surface of Mars. *Mariner 9* could only take pictures of the dust clouds.

Over time, the dust storm stopped. The spacecraft began taking more pictures as soon as the dust cleared. *Mariner 9* discovered many features on Mars. It took pictures of deep valleys and giant volcanoes. It found channels on Mars that looked like dried-up streams or rivers. *Mariner 9* also took pictures of marks left on the surface by strong windstorms.

The pictures from the *Mariner* missions helped astronomers learn what the surface of Mars looks like. Astronomers also studied the *Mariner* pictures to find places to land future spacecraft.

▲ This picture from *Viking* shows the rocks and the orange-pink sky of Mars.

Viking Space Probes

The United States launched two spacecraft to Mars in 1975. These spacecraft were *Viking 1* and *Viking 2*. Each Viking spacecraft had two parts. The first part was a large spacecraft built to orbit Mars. The second part was a lander. The lander was built to drop down from the orbiting spacecraft and land on the surface of Mars. The *Viking* missions were the first to place landers on Mars.

The *Viking* spacecraft began to orbit Mars in 1976. They took pictures of Mars and sent them to Earth. Scientists looked at the pictures and found places for the landers to touch down. Mission controllers released the landers one month after the spacecraft began to orbit. Mission controllers operate spacecraft from Earth.

The landers fell toward Mars. They landed about one month apart and 4,000 miles (6,437 km) away from each other.

Each *Viking* lander had two cameras that took pictures and sent them back to Earth. The landers had instruments to check the weather and the soil on Mars. They had machines to measure any movement, such as earthquakes, on the surface of Mars.

Each lander also had a robotic arm. Mission controllers sent commands from Earth to the lander. The landers did what the controllers instructed. They used their robotic arms to scoop up Martian soil. The *Viking* landers checked the soil for living things. Scientists disagree about the results of the *Viking* tests. Some believe there were signs of life. Others do not think there were signs of life.

Sojourner studied Mars rocks and soil samples.

Mars *Pathfinder*

In 1997, the United States sent *Pathfinder* into space. *Pathfinder* carried a rover called *Sojourner*. The rover was a small robot car. Scientists sent instructions to *Sojourner* from Earth.

Pathfinder landed on Mars on July 4, 1997. Huge airbags filled with air and surrounded the spacecraft when it landed. *Pathfinder* bounced twice when it hit the surface. The airbags protected the spacecraft during this bumpy landing.

After *Pathfinder* stopped moving, mission controllers let the air out of the bags. *Pathfinder's* instruments began measuring the weather. Its cameras sent pictures back to Earth.

Mission controllers opened *Pathfinder's* petal-like doors. A ramp unrolled. Mission controllers steered the rover down the ramp and onto the planet's surface. Then they moved the rover around rocks and over the surface of Mars.

Sojourner had spiked wheels, so it could travel through the soil on Mars. It carried tools to study rocks. The instruments measured what the rocks were made of. *Sojourner* and *Pathfinder* worked for 90 days until they ran out of power. Scientists are still studying the information they gathered.

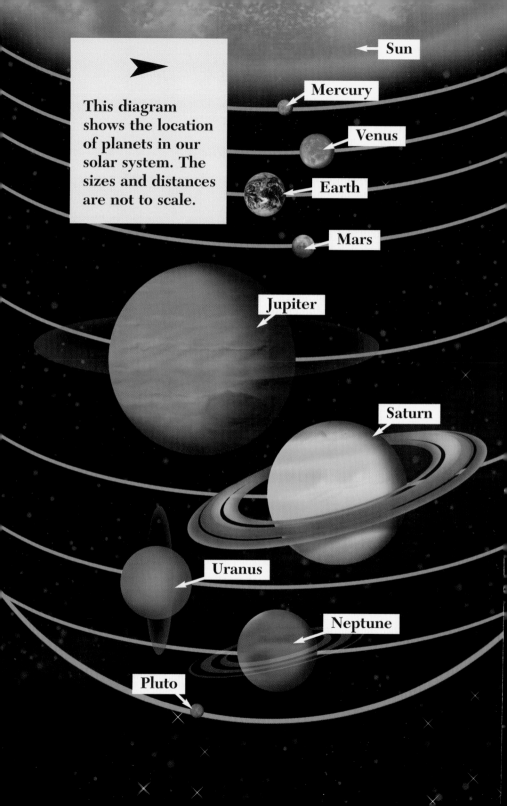

This diagram shows the location of planets in our solar system. The sizes and distances are not to scale.

Sun

Mercury

Venus

Earth

Mars

Jupiter

Saturn

Uranus

Neptune

Pluto

Outer Solar System

Four giant planets orbit far from the Sun in the outer solar system. Jupiter, Saturn, Uranus, and Neptune are millions of miles away from the Sun. It takes special explorer space probes to reach these planets.

The outer solar system is so far away that a rocket would not be able to carry the space probes far enough. The rocket would run out of fuel long before it reached these planets.

Scientists use a planet's gravity to help steer the space probes. Gravity is a force that attracts objects to each other. When a probe comes close to a planet, the planet's gravity pulls on it. This speeds up the probe. It also pulls the probe into a path that curves around the planet. Scientists use this curving to change a space probe's path. That way, the space probe can visit other planets.

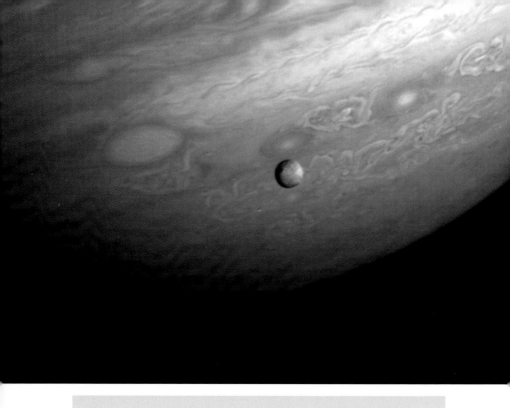

As *Voyager 2* passed Jupiter, it took this picture of the planet and its moon Io.

Pioneer Missions

In 1972 and 1973, astronomers launched the *Pioneer 10* and *Pioneer 11* space probes. These probes flew near Jupiter in December 1973 and December 1974. They were the first space probes to fly by Jupiter. *Pioneer 10* then continued on its way out of the solar system. In 1983, it became the first spacecraft sent beyond the solar system. *Pioneer 11* flew by Saturn in September 1979.

Voyager Space Probes

In 1977, U.S. scientists launched the *Voyager 1* and *Voyager 2* space probes. Each *Voyager* spacecraft has a large dish-shaped antenna. Below the antenna is a box that carries scientific instruments. Each spacecraft has two television cameras and tools for measuring temperatures. They also have antennas for sending information to Earth. The spacecraft have special batteries that are designed to provide power for many years. Each *Voyager* also has small rockets to change its course.

It took the *Voyager* probes almost two years of traveling to reach Jupiter. Each visited Jupiter in 1979. They passed the giant planet, taking pictures and measurements. Jupiter's gravity redirected the probes. They were sent into space toward Saturn. They circled Saturn and took pictures. Then *Voyager 1* flew by Saturn's moons to take close-up pictures. *Voyager 2* traveled from Saturn to Uranus and then on to Neptune.

The *Voyager* probes are on their way out of the solar system. As long as they work, the probes will continue to send information about deep space to Earth. Scientists expect both *Voyagers* to continue working until 2030. At that time, they will run out of power.

Voyager Discoveries

Scientists learned many things by studying information from the *Voyager* spacecraft. These space probes gave scientists their first close-up views of Jupiter, Saturn, Uranus, and Neptune.

Scientists learned much about Jupiter. They learned that hurricanelike storms swirl in Jupiter's atmosphere. They discovered that different colored clouds that circle the planet give Jupiter its striped appearance. The probes found three faint rings around Jupiter. They also found erupting volcanoes on Jupiter's moon Io.

Voyager 1 flew by Saturn in 1980 and *Voyager 2* passed by in 1981. The probes took pictures of Saturn's rings. The rings look solid from Earth. But close-up pictures showed that the rings are made of tiny bits of rock, ice, and dust. The large rings are made up of thousands of small rings. They look like the lines on a compact disk.

Voyager 2 flew by Uranus in 1986. It found several moons orbiting the planet.

In 1989, *Voyager 2* flew by Neptune. It took pictures of Neptune and observed a large storm with swirling winds. It studied Neptune's moon Triton and found that it was one the coldest places in the solar system.

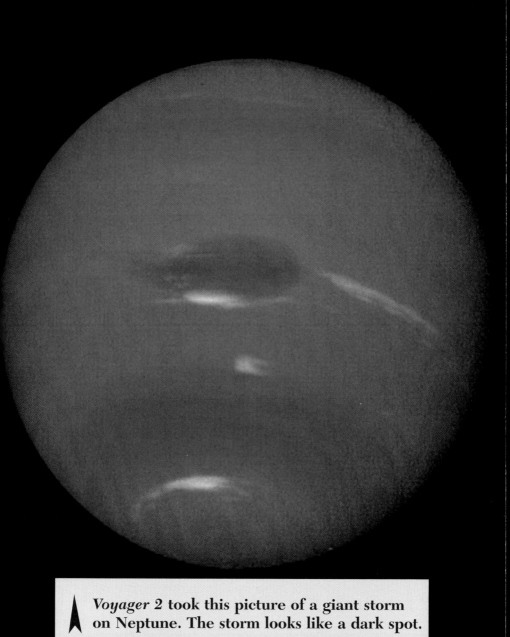

Voyager 2 took this picture of a giant storm on Neptune. The storm looks like a dark spot.

In this picture, astronauts are working on the Hubble Space Telescope.

Deep Space

No space probe has ever been to the planet Pluto, the farthest planet from the Sun. Scientists would like to send a probe, but the trip would take 12 years or more. For now, scientists are using telescopes to explore Pluto. Telescopes make faraway objects look clearer and closer.

Some telescopes that have studied Pluto are on spacecraft. The Hubble Space Telescope is a telescope that orbits Earth. The HST looks at objects using the same light as people see. But other explorer spacecraft take pictures by using energy rays that are invisible to people. For example, the Chandra X-ray Observatory looks at objects with X-rays. Other spacecraft use radio waves to look at objects in space.

The Hubble Space Telescope took this picture of a distant galaxy.

Distant Objects

Telescopes on spacecraft examine deep space. Objects in deep space appear unclear in telescopes on Earth. This is because Earth's hazy atmosphere blocks some of the light and makes the view fuzzy.

Objects in deep space are also hard to see because they are so far away from Earth. The nearest star to our Sun is billions of miles away. Most objects in space are even farther away.

Space telescopes are making many new discoveries. They have found stars of all sizes and colors. Some stars have planets that circle around them.

Scientists have found many new groups of stars using space telescopes. Sometimes a group is only a few dozen stars. Other times, thousands or even millions of stars cluster together. A galaxy is a very large system of stars and objects that orbit the stars. Gravity holds the galaxy together. Earth and the Sun are part of the Milky Way Galaxy. This galaxy has more than 100 billion stars.

Scientists use telescopes to study how planets and stars form. These objects form in colorful clouds of gas and dust called nebulas. Telescopes also watch how stars die. By studying this information, scientists are learning about how our solar system formed and what the future of Earth may be.

This is an artist's idea of what the *Cassini* spacecraft will look like as it lands on Titan.

Future Explorers

Each time an explorer space probe visits a planet, scientists make new discoveries. Each discovery causes scientists to ask more questions. New spacecraft are needed to gather more information so scientists can answer their questions.

Some new spacecraft are already on their way to the gas giants. The *Cassini* spacecraft is traveling to Saturn. It is carrying a small capsule that will land on Saturn's moon Titan.

The *Messenger* spacecraft is being developed to go to Mercury. It will be the first spacecraft to visit Mercury since *Mariner 10* in 1974.

Many space missions are still in the planning stage. Scientists want to send a probe on a deep space mission to Pluto. The European Space Agency is planning to build new space telescopes. The Darwin Project is planning to link six Hubble-sized telescopes together. The telescopes will work like one giant telescope that is more powerful than the Hubble.

Astronomers are planning new missions for astronauts, too. Scientists are working on ways to send humans to Mars. Some people believe the first human explorers on Mars may arrive there in the next 20 or 30 years. As long as there are questions about space, people will try to explore it.

Glossary

astronomer (ah-STRAHN-uh-mur)—a scientist who studies objects in space

atmosphere (AT-muh-sfear)—a layer of gases that surrounds an object in space

crater (KRAY-tur)—a bowl-shaped hole left when a meteorite strikes an object in space

galaxy (GAL-uhk-see)—a very large system of nebulas, stars, and objects orbiting them that is held together by gravity

meteorite (MEE-tee-ur-rite)—a rock from outer space that crashes into a planet or moon's surface

missile (MISS-uhl)—a rocket that carries a weapon, spacecraft, or other payload

orbit (OR-bit)—the path an object takes around another object in space

rocket (ROK-it)—a tube-shaped vehicle with a pointed end that can travel very fast

satellite (SAT-uh-lite)—a spacecraft sent into space to circle Earth; some satellites take pictures or record information about Earth.

solar system (SOH-lur SISS-tuhm)—the Sun and all the objects that orbit it

NASA for Kids
http://kids.msfc.nasa.gov

NASA Office of Space Flight
http://www.hq.nasa.gov/osf/

**Star Child: A Learning Center for
  Young Astronomers**
http://starchild.gsfc.nasa.gov/docs/StarChild/
  StarChild.html

Astronomical Society of the Pacific
390 Ashton Avenue
San Francisco, CA 94112

NASA Headquarters
Washington, DC 20546-0001

Index